A FAR GREEN COUNTRY

BRIAN LOVETT

Copyright © 2015 Brian Lovett

All rights reserved.

ISBN: 1517144523
ISBN-13: 978-1517144524

DEDICATION

To all the great turkey folks who have helped me along this path.
And Jenny. Especially Jenny.

CONTENTS

Acknowledgments

1	The Trade	3
2	A Bird Apart	9
3	An Accidental Yelper	16
4	Chasing Blue Sky	21
5	A Fool's Fortnight	26
6	Greasing the Hand of Fate	32
7	Moonlight Mile	36
8	This Shabby Swindler	41
9	Dead Leaves and the Dirty Ground	46
10	The Gobbler	50
11	A Far Green Country	58

ACKNOWLEDGMENTS

Thanks go out to:
Tes Randle Jolly for the gorgeous cover photo.
Jen West for serving as my editor.
Al West for the wonderful cover design.
And Karen Lee, Matt Lindler and all the great folks at the National Wild Turkey Federation.

INTRODUCTION

Sometime in 1991, I wrote my first newspaper column about turkey hunting. I'd guess that almost everyone who read the piece has long forgotten it. I recall it, however, because it was awful. I basically wrote myself into a corner while trying to compare the merits of turkey hunting to those of waterfowling, deer hunting and other outdoors pursuits. When I was almost finished, I realized the article was boring and juvenile. But the weekly outdoors page deadline loomed, so I touched up the story as best I could and went with it. Thankfully, readers were too polite to point out that I'd wasted their time.

I set myself up for that failure, as I'd only hunted turkeys two mornings in my life. Both outings had occurred the previous spring and were laughable. Technically, I was turkey hunting, but in reality, I was just bumbling around a Crawford County, Wis., coulee while toting a shotgun. That lack of appreciation for and experience with turkey hunting was reflected in that forgettable newspaper column.

I can forgive myself now. At the time, I didn't realize the hold turkey hunting takes on the hearts and minds of its true believers. Nowadays, that's a constant part of my existence. Obsession might best describe it, but many folks obsess about this or that and then quickly turn their thoughts elsewhere. Addiction is an appropriate term, but I typically shy away from that word because it indicates an unhealthy dependence on something. Turkey hunting too much at the expense of faith, family and career can be unhealthy, but generally, time in the turkey woods is uplifting and therapeutic.

Devotion? That certainly applies, as true turkey hunters pursue their passion and its various skill sets year-round, even forsaking other outdoor activities when there's one last tag to fill. Maybe one-word descriptions don't suffice. We'll just agree that for the faithful, turkeys and turkey hunting grasp your interest, mind and heart like no other wild animal or pursuit.

Which brought me to the chapters here. This loose collection of musings isn't intended to be a turkey hunting guide. I've written plenty of those, and honestly, I don't know if I could do another. This is just a sample of memories, reflections and a few episodes from 25 years of passionate, obsessive and, sure, addictive devotion to chasing the wild turkey. A lot has changed since that weekend of so-called turkey hunting in 1990, though at times, I still feel like I'm doing nothing more than bumbling around the woods while toting a shotgun. But succeed or fail, I'm really just trying to wring another hour or episode from everything turkey hunting offers. Like all of us, I'm forever seeking that far green country.

— *Brian Lovett, February 2015*

1 THE TRADE

You sit up and stare blankly at the alarm. 2:45 a.m. Yeah, you could sleep 15 more minutes, but why bother at this point? Besides, being early never hurts.

Stumbling down the hall, you peek in the den and confirm that the dog is curled up in deep slumber. Smart pooch. You try to formulate some witty thought about a Labrador being wiser than a human, but you're too damn tired to think about anything but coffee.

How long has it been now, the streak of dark-thirty wake-up calls? Four weeks? Five weeks? You can't remember. It doesn't matter. It's been long enough to turn you into a sleep-deprived zombie but brief enough to leave you lusting for more. Days off would be nice — even welcomed. But the season grows short, and spring wanes. You'll have plenty of restful mornings when June's heat envelops the landscape and the smell of the first alfalfa cutting rides on a westerly wind.

You creep down the stairs, careful not to make too much commotion, and grab your boots and vest. The gun will have to wait for a second trip. When everything is assembled by the front door, you grab your coffee mug, load the truck, lock the house and slip away into the night.

And make no mistake, it's still night. You drive down empty streets, chuckling softly because the only fools awake at this hour are drunks and turkey hunters. Mock them if you will, but at least the drunks might get some decent sleep later.

The drive passes quickly. It always does, as your mind typically races with memories of the past few mornings and plans for the day. You have a hundred what-ifs to consider, and many of those quandaries don't have easy answers. You'd planned to listen from the town road and go to the first gobbler that sounded off. But if a bird bellowed from the eastern woods, you'd have quite a walk.

Would it make more sense to cut across the big pasture and wait at the edge of the eastern woods? It's always a coin flip. And even as you remind yourself that you cannot be in two places at once, you crave surety that will make your decision easier.

Soon, you're standing at the pasture gate, running all those scenarios through your head again. Ah, to heck with it. You'll go all in at the eastern woods. Only by doing so, sarcasm suggests, will you ensure that turkeys will light up across the road to the west.

The walk in is always a bit unsettling. The humid morning chill catches you by surprise. It will fade quickly during your morning aerobics but usually returns after you've sat by a tree for a while. And although you've been to this place dozens of times, it's still black out, and you're navigating more by memory than visual confirmation. You can't afford to daydream, either. Silence and stealth are your allies, and this is the time to practice them. An unseen twig or, worse, electric fence might not end your morning, but it will sure put a damper on it.

Finally at your listening spot, you lean back against a broad white oak and shut your eyes for a moment of rest and peace. Gobbling won't begin for another 15 or 20 minutes, and you've earned the respite. The woods usually seem absolutely silent during these predawn waits, broken only now and then by the soft footsteps of nearby deer or a streaking whir of duck wings overhead. Soon, songbirds begin to stir, and a cardinal — always a cardinal — sounds off. The action is just minutes away, and your ears strain to catch and course that first gobble.

There! To the south. Or was it more southwest? Another gobble confirms the latter, and your hunter's mind begins to churn. The turkey is on the neighbor's property, and you're nowhere near close enough to work him. If you're quick yet quiet, you might have time to slip along the edge of the hardwoods, through the young pine thicket and into the small finger of woods that borders the fence line. You've called turkeys there twice before and know the spot well. It could work.

You ease back west over the small ridge and carefully try to pick your steps south to the fence row. The leaves crunch and pop like cornflakes in the still morning air, and you curse your clumsiness. Just a few more yards, though, and you will have reached the relative security of the pines. Stopping briefly, you wait to hear another gobble — proof, perhaps, that the turkey hasn't heard your movement. When it finally echoes across the pasture, you're off again, determined to reach the fence.

Made it. You're relieved, but it's no time to pat yourself on the back. You have 100 yards of pines to navigate before attempting to slip or crawl into the tiny hardwood finger. With daylight and fly-down time beckoning, time is critical.

The pines pass quickly, and you're soon at the spit of woods. It's unlikely the turkey can see you, but you take no chances. As your knees and elbows sink into the dew-soaked grass, you strain to move your body a few more yards to an ash tree about 15 steps into the woods. Although it doesn't seem that difficult, you're huffing and puffing when you reach the tree and plop your butt on your cushion. Time for business.

The gobbler is now on the ground, no doubt. Gripping a time-worn slate in your shaking left hand, you eke out a few soft yelps and wait for a response. The bird is right on time, uttering a chortling gobble from the wooded flat 100-some yards in front of you. Ignoring your own best advice, you yelp again, and the bird hammers back.

It's then the mental reminders begin. "Stay focused. Watch for him," you think. "Keep your gun at the ready. Don't be impatient." This is Turkey 101, of course, but you refresh yourself every time, every turkey, to avoid rookie blunders. There's enough that can go wrong. You don't need to be part of the problem.

Confident and ready, you cluck lightly and follow it up with some yelping. Nothing. You yelp again, a bit louder and with more urgency. Silence. Hmm. There's no sense calling to an unresponsive turkey, you remind yourself, so you set the call down for a minute to wait and listen. Just as you're about to reach for it again, the turkey gobbles on his own — from the same spot.

So, it'll be one of those hunts. With a field behind you and the property line 40 steps in front of you, moving is out of the question. The bird will have to come to you. Or, more precisely, you'll have to be patient and give the turkey a reason to come to you. This is the game you'll play.

A string of yelps on your slate brings another lusty gobble from the turkey, but he still hasn't moved. You follow the yelping with cutting and more yelping on a glass call. Again, more gobbling but no movement. Switching back to the slate, you yelp and cutt some more — cue the gobbling — but then set the calls down and vow to be quiet for several minutes. This excite-then-ignore tactic often prompts a stubborn gobbler to leave his line in the sand and search for the hen he's heard. Other times, of course, it just makes him gobble and dig his feet in harder.

This day, he's chosen the latter. He'll gobble at anything you throw at him but probably hasn't moved 10 feet. He's with a hen, no doubt. They often are. It's breeding season, after all, so that's not unusual. At some point during the day, he probably won't have female company, but you'll never know when that might occur. It could be five minutes from now, or it might not be until this afternoon. Where will you be when he's lonely and more vulnerable? That, too, is unknown.

But for now, you're near him and in contact. Better, you have some time to wait. So you switch tactics, calling here and there, and then throwing in long periods of silence to hopefully play on the gobbler's curiosity. And for an hour or two, it works well enough. The bird gobbles here and there, aware of your calling but unwilling to budge.

Eventually, your comfort level starts to diminish. Not only are you losing faith in your approach and chances, but your foot is numb, your butt is aching and you really need to lose a layer of clothing. Oh, and you're more than a bit curious and concerned about whatever is crawling around on your neck. Yet the contest continues, so you press on.

A yelp after 10 minutes of quiet sparks an immediate gobble. Wait now. That actually seemed a bit closer. Vowing not to get too excited, you wait a couple of minutes and then call softly again. Another gobble filters through the timber, and yes, it's closer, if only perhaps by a few yards. Maybe the gobbler is just following a hen as she pecks around the flat, but it's possible that he's slowly approaching your setup. Suddenly, fatigue becomes a memory, and discomfort is ignored. Pure focus on that turkey consumes your being.

Even now, there's the heartbeat. No, it's not like the pounding, almost audible heartbeat you experienced years ago during your first turkey encounters — the one that threatened to leave you gasping for air and unable to finish the deal. This pulse is a bit more subdued but still formidable. It rises from your gut and surges through your neck. You feel your breath quicken a bit, even as you subconsciously tell your body to calm down. You won't lose this feeling, no matter how many gobblers you face. After a while, you just learn to get past it until the hunt is finished and you can exhale.

But about that hunt. Something's not right. While you were getting excited by the turkey's possible approach, the bird seems to have clammed up. He could be coming in, of course, as they often go silent when they walk. Still, this seems different. Seconds later, you hear soft crunching and strain your eyes toward the source. There's a flicker of movement by a pine, but something's amiss. Long, low and swift, this is no turkey. It's a coyote. And in a second, he zips past your gaze and into a thicket. The silence makes sense now. Your calling and the turkey's gobbling attracted the dog, and he probably spooked the longbeard when he slipped in for a look. You wait and call for a few minutes just in case that's not true, but further silence confirms it. Your hunt — that long, gut-wrenching chess match — is finished.

You have no worries about the turkey. He's fine. In fact, he might even resume gobbling in a bit. But after three long hours on your buttpad, you're late for work and need to leave him. He'll have to wait for another day, if you are fortunate enough to contact him again.

Rising, you stretch, gather your calls and begin the long walk back to the truck. The midmorning sun shines on your neck, and for the first time in a while, you're hot. Your feet, trapped in wool socks and rubber boots designed to repel the morning chill, beg for release. By the time you reach your vehicle, they're sore.

The prospect of a day at work after too little sleep and a tiring early morning makes you wince. It sure would be nice to nap. Better, a night of normal slumber would replenish your body and refresh your mind, making you feel almost human again. But with a week and a half left in the season, those thoughts will wait. You have other farms, more turkeys and unrealized adventures to uncover. You have so many calls to run, so many strategies to implement and so few hours in which to do so. To an outsider, this breakneck lifestyle in pursuit of a black bird might seem pointless or even absurd. But that's the deal you made, man. This is your trade. You chose the lifestyle the second you gasped at that first gobble decades ago, and you could no more give it up now than you could stop breathing.

Fatigue and comfort be damned. Onward through the end of spring. No brakes. You might not kill another turkey this season, but you'll sure hunt them. Ultimately, memories and reflections of that pursuit and the difficulties it entails will prove to be your greatest reward.

* * *

2 A BIRD APART

They say youth is wasted on the young, and so, I'm afraid, was the first wild turkey I ever saw.

Turkeys had been extirpated from my native Wisconsin for almost a century, so seeing one in the early 1980s was a pretty big deal. One October day, my father, brother, a friend and I had been grouse hunting at a large wildlife area and were driving to another spot when a family flock of hens and poults crossed the road. My dad immediately stopped the car and pointed out the birds, marveling at them as if they were dinosaurs. I was curious but not overwhelmed, lacking any perspective about the swift decline of turkeys in America and the overwhelming resurgence to come. So when the group sprinted into the ditch and disappeared in some brush, the thought of turkeys pretty much left my mind for years.

Technically, those were really not even native Eastern turkeys. They were the descendants of 7/8 wild Allegheny-strain birds that had been raised at a Pennsylvania game farm and then released into the massive Meadow Valley Wildlife Area and adjacent Necedah National Wildlife Refuge in central Wisconsin during the mid-1950s. That effort was an early attempt at wild turkey restoration in Wisconsin, and although it worked well enough for the state to hold three limited seasons in the late 1960s, the population eventually failed. Only a few birds from that bloodline remained in that area during my childhood.

At the time, I didn't realize that a much broader, more intelligent restoration effort was already underway in southwestern Wisconsin.

Building off trap-and-transplant successes in other states, Wisconsin had traded ruffed grouse to Missouri in exchange for Eastern turkeys, and then released them in what was believed to be suitable habitat. I don't need to tell you what happened. Turkey populations grew steadily — even exploded — and the birds became probably the top wildlife restoration success story in American history.

Several years after seeing the almost-wild turkeys, I walked along a fence line in Crawford County, Wis., and witnessed my first true wild Eastern. The hen flushed from a brushy spot — probably off a nest, but I wouldn't realize that until years later — hovered for a second in the wind and then sailed into a deep valley pasture. Later that day, while driving around the area, I saw my first strutter, and the next morning, I heard my first gobbles.

I wouldn't see or touch my first dead turkey for a few seasons. My inexperience and utter lack of turkey hunting knowledge saw to that. But when a friend finally shot a gobbler at a small central Wisconsin woodlot one April, I experienced firsthand the close-up miracle of the wild turkey. It was so different than the birds of my youth — ducks, grouse, geese, pheasants, woodcock and pigeons. The black feathers seemed to shine like obsidian reflecting a roaring blaze, and the brilliant red, white and blue of the gobbler's head, even fading in death, burned into my mind. I marveled at the bird's muddy feet and sharp spurs, but the wattles and snood fascinated me. I'd never seen or touched anything like them. What purpose did they serve? Why did no other bird have them?

I shot my first gobbler the next morning, sitting at the same spot where my friend had scored. In the interest of full disclosure, I shot it four times. The first shot, at 12 steps, killed it, but I'd never seen a dead gobbler flop before, and my inner duck hunter kept screaming to pull the trigger. I did, and when the pellets stopped flying, I had one very dead turkey. Amazed by every facet of the bird, I plucked and roasted the meat, and made my first attempt at a fan and beard mount, which didn't turn out too bad. It still hangs in my basement today. Don't ask me why, but I only kept one leg from the 2-year-old gobbler. I guess I didn't realize the significance of spurs then. I have remedied that, as the current scene in my basement workroom indicates.

Those early experiences marked the first steps in my lifelong fascination with the world's greatest game bird. Almost three decades later, the sight, sound and feel of a wild turkey gobbler thrills me almost as much as when I was a neophyte. And that holds true for birds and subspecies across the country. Although I mostly discuss Easterns here, the descriptions hold true for the other four subspecies of *Meleagris gallopavo*: Gould's, Osceola, Merriam's and Rio Grande. True, each subspecies has minor physiological differences from the others, such as the length of their legs, the size of their body frames or the color of their covert feathers. And their voices might differ somewhat, especially with the relatively light-gobbling Gould's, Merriam's and Rio Grandes. However, they remain birds of a feather, and the enchantment they weave doesn't vary from Mexico to Ontario, Maine to California. The bird's physical makeup is remarkable, with an amazingly intricate mosaic of body feathers, deceptively powerful and effective flight feathers, and almost delicately arrayed tail feathers. Another unique collection of feathers, the beard, defies description. A collection of hair-like bristles, or filaments, protrudes from the chest of a gobbler (and about 5 percent of hens) and gives an individual bird much of its character. Some beards are straight, yet others are curved or even somewhat hooked, as if they've taken a set from a curling iron. Many are broad and thick, yet others are thin and seemingly spindly.

And then there's the head, which, to me, is the most interesting part of a turkey. There is no more thrilling sight in hunting than seeing the unmistakable lightbulb-white noggin of a gobbler bobbing as it weaves through the woods toward you. Depending on the turkey and its mood, the wattles and neck might glow blood-red while the sides of the head show brilliant blue. The snood — defined as a fleshy erectile protuberance — at the base of the bird's beak might hang limp as the turkey struts and then grow erect as the bird slicks down its feathers and drops out of strut. The eyes — those dark, all-seeing eyes — seem to bore a hole in you. Whether they belong to a brilliant gobbler or dull-colored hen, the eyes get me. They see every movement and seem to judge your intentions. There is no defeating them.

But perhaps it's sound that best defines my fascination with turkeys. They are a vocal bird, though not quite in the manner of geese or cranes. Their vocabulary is broad and varied — so much that even after decades of study, we do not fully comprehend or understand it. Yet that lexicon — and other sounds — defines the way in which we interact with and pursue turkeys. We spend hundreds of hours trying to memorize and mimic the yelps, clucks, cackling, cutting, whistling and purring of hens. We marvel at the soft whistles and whines we can only hear when birds are close. Likewise, we strain our ears to hear spitting and drumming — that deep, reverberating sound gobblers muster up from their chests. And we chuckle at the sometimes ridiculous noises and calling attempts of young turkeys, especially jakes.

The sound foremost in our thoughts and souls, of course, is the gobble, which lets us know the whereabouts and sometimes mood and intentions of a male turkey. Many hunters have tried to describe it, and most fall short. It's primal and guttural, with a distinct resonance. The sound varies greatly from the powerful echo of a gobble in deep timber to the lighter, more ethereal sound of a gobble floating along prairie breezes. Depending on the situation, its savagery might startle and even scare you. A gobble from a turkey within 50 yards is incredibly unnerving, as you can hear every detail of the sound, including the rattle from deep within the bird's throat, which seems powerful enough to rattle the bird apart. Drumming and the sound of your own heart thumping will follow, and the hunt will likely reach a quick conclusion.

Turkeys have another fascinating feature that we often overlook: their personalities. Now, don't get me wrong. I don't contend that they show personality traits like dogs, and I'm not about to suggest they're anything like humans. In truth, many of the personality elements they exhibit are merely behaviors we observe, interpret and sometimes embellish. Still, birds are individuals, and they often act differently from each other. Some are eager, yet others seem shy. Many are loud, but others are quiet. A few are aggressive, and others seem passive or even submissive. Some gobblers walk and strut with a sturdy posture and gait that screams confidence or arrogance. Others poke their head up every five seconds to check out the unseen bogeyman in the woods. Many hens pay no attention to calling or decoys as they feed or walk past, yet others become so agitated and vocal that you'd swear your calling had insulted them. Only in one aspect do turkeys never waver: their reaction to any perceived danger. They have no curiosity; only evolution-honed survival instinct. Whether they walk, run or fly in retreat, they will not stick around when they sense a threat. We hate and love them for that, as their inherent paranoia makes hunting difficult but ensures there will be turkeys for generations to come.

One final aspect of turkeys and turkey hunting always mystifies me. That is, it sticks in my craw. It's the manner in which a few folks view the bird, trying to make trophies out of some gobblers while diminishing others. I dislike this intensely, as it lessens the turkey hunting experience. My view on this doesn't change: Any gobbler killed in a clean, legal and ethical manner is a trophy. I don't care if the bird is 2 or 5. Turkey hunting revolves around the bird and the pursuit, not the relative merits of a gobbler's weight, beard or spurs.

Some folks argue otherwise, and I see their point. A paintbrush beard or 1-1/2-inch hooks look more impressive in post-hunt photos than a pencil-thin beard and rounded spurs. The critical words are *post-hunt*. Those "trophy" aspects are only considerations after a gobbler is flopping. In fact, some are dubious at best, and most are impossible to identify during typical hunting conditions.

Show me someone who claims he can accurately judge the weight of a live gobbler, and I'll show you a liar. Every gobbler looks large, especially if it struts. Only when turkeys are side by side can you determine the relative size of one gobbler versus another. What's more, the amount of breast sponge — the fatty layer atop a turkey's breast — can account for a large percentage of a bird's weight. There's no way of determining that until you clean a gobbler. I've witnessed doubles on turkeys — likely siblings — that varied greatly in weight. One might be 23 pounds and the other 17, yet both appeared identical in life and post-hunt photographs. Unless one gobbler stands considerably taller and broader than others nearby, you simply cannot judge its relative weight.

And the beard? Sure, if two gobblers appear together, one might have a beard that's longer than the other's. Trouble is, those birds, again, are likely siblings, and the longer beard probably gained "trophy" status thanks to chance or the genetic lottery. Most beards don't vary much, usually measuring 8-1/2 to 10-1/2 inches. True, they grow 4 to 5 inches per year throughout a gobbler's life, but the tips constantly break or rub off when a gobbler stoops to feed or squats on the roost. Beards are only a good determinant of age until a bird is 3. Spring jakes usually have 3- to 4-inch beards, though some early-hatched birds sport 5-inch beards. When a gobbler reaches 2, his beard is usually 8 to 10 inches. A beard gets its black color from melanin, a pigment that colors and strengthens feathers. The newly emerging beards of young turkeys contain little melanin, so the bristles are amber-colored. Even when a gobbler is 2, his beard will retain those original amber tips because they haven't broken off yet. If you hold the beard of a 2-year-old gobbler under light, you'll see the tips are mostly amber. When a gobbler is 3, his beard will have grown about 14 inches. But again, few toms have beards that long because the bristles wear off at the tip at about the same rate as the beard grows. Therefore, most 3-year-old and older gobblers have "only" 9- to 10-inch beards, and the tips will be mostly black because the original amber filaments have broken off.

Don't get me started on spurs. Yes, they're by far the most reliable indication of a gobbler's age. Conventional wisdom holds that 2-year-olds have rounded spurs that are typically 3/4 to 7/8 inches, 3-year-olds have sharper, curved hooks that measure at least 1 inch, 4-year-olds have sharp hooks that exceed 1-3/8 inches, and 5-year-olds have 1-1/2-inch-plus hooks. That's not absolute, as studies have shown spur length exhibits substantial variation as it corresponds to age. Still, I think everyone would agree that long, sharp, curved hooks indicate older birds. Just don't tell me you gauge spur length while hunting. I guess some folks might have the luxury of examining the legs of gobblers at close range to judge hooks. But unless you own thousands of acres of unhunted ground and have the vision of a fighter pilot, that scenario isn't realistic. In fact, it's silly. In 99 percent of hunting situations, when a gobbler offers you a good shot, you take it. Only when you stand over the bird do you know its spur length.

Some hunters maintain they can determine the relative age of turkeys by their gobble or behavior. There might be something to this. A 2-year-old's gobble is often slightly higher-pitched, and an older turkey's gobble has a deeper chortle. However, such determinations are never definitive. They're just guesses or even hunches. Likewise, a bird's demeanor or actions might indicate it's an older turkey. Two-year-olds, after all, often gobble more and come to calling more eagerly than older turkeys. And old gobblers can be quiet, henned-up pains in the butt. But again, that's never absolute. I've shot henned-up 2-year-olds that acted like the king of the woods, and I've had long-spurred old turkeys sprint in after one series of yelps. The behavior of any gobbler usually hinges on its mood and the situation.

I guess that rant is a long way of saying any gobbler should be held in high regard. The hunt is the trophy. After you shoot, the bird is really reduced to a pile of feathers and meat. Post-hunt examinations of the gobbler's weight, beard and spurs say nothing about the turkey's stirring gobble, the calling and chess match required to kill the bird or the heart-pounding moment when the brilliant head and crimson body popped into view. A long, broad beard and razor-sharp hooks are impressive, but they're only one part of a greater story.

I'm sure my respect and wonder for turkeys will grow and change as I continue along the hunting path. Hopefully, I'm only halfway through my turkey hunting career and will be allowed to experience these birds for decades to come. Though it often seems that I attempt to kill every gobbler in the woods, I'd sacrifice all of that to ensure that turkeys remained on the landscape forever. The hunting, after all, is just a facet of the enchantment cast over me by a miraculous animal. Here's hoping that spell — the almost hypnotic fascination with a bird — never ends or wanes. If it does, I'll quit, for I'll have lost sight of everything important in turkey hunting.

* * *

3 AN ACCIDENTAL YELPER

There was a day when normalcy prevailed and my ears didn't ring.

That was 25-plus years ago, before the little brown snuff can and the cassette tape found their way into my house — before I took the first steps down the long path of trying to replicate the vocabulary of the wild turkey.

The snuff can contained three Quaker Boy mouth calls, stretched and recommended by inimitable caller Dick Kirby. And the audiotape featured calling instruction and the recording of an actual hunt from the master yelper himself — five-time World champion Ben Rogers Lee. Both were gifts from my father about the time we received our first permits to hunt spring turkeys in our home state of Wisconsin. We knew nothing about turkey hunting, of course, and even less about turkey calling. But with instruction from two calling legends, what could go wrong?

Every day after work, I'd insert the tape in a small cassette player and pop a diaphragm in my mouth. The first several attempts were predictably hilarious. At first, I couldn't produce any sound. Then, if I huffed and puffed to the point of having a stroke, I could make sort of a raspy scream/whistle, which, of course, sounded nothing like the noises I heard Lee making on the tape. In fact, I don't think they resembled anything in nature.

Vowing to improve, I referred to the literature that had come folded in the snuff box. To yelp, it suggested, you should huff air from your diaphragm while mouthing the word "thee-ock." That was an epiphany. The next few weeks, I thee-ocked my way around the house, still sounding nothing like Lee but improving, at least in my mind.

Around that time, a friend mentioned he knew a guy at work who was pretty good at turkey calling. I responded that I'd become fairly skilled and offered to demonstrate. I popped the three-reed Quaker Boy in my mouth and ripped off a series of thee-ocks.

I will never forget the look on his face and his response.

"Um ... no."

With that candid criticism, I realized that I stunk. And no matter how hard I tried, I couldn't seem to get better. So the first three or four years I hunted, I didn't call much. In fact, when I finally killed my first gobbler, I didn't call at all. I simply waited all morning at the corner of a field where my buddy — the same one who recoiled at my calling — had killed a turkey the previous day. The next year, without calling, we killed two more turkeys at that spot, and I began to suspect calling was overrated. I thought back to my duck hunting experience the previous 10 years, during which I'd been reasonably successful without calling much. At that time, conventional wisdom in waterfowling held that 90 percent of hunters didn't have the skill or experience to call well enough to bend ducks to their will. As such, most of their calling efforts were wasted or even counterproductive. Turkey hunting, I reasoned in my limited experience, must be the same.

But about that time, I got my first big break in the outdoors industry: editing a Wisconsin hunting and fishing magazine. One of the magazine's sister publications was a turkey hunting magazine, and I soon met several folks who were — not astonishingly — much better turkey hunters and callers than I was. These veterans politely but quickly debunked my belief that calling was not important and encouraged me to practice while listening to audiotapes of real turkeys. These, of course, were cleverly titled *Real Turkeys*, and were recorded and produced by the great Lovett E. Williams Jr.

Suddenly, my calling horizons expanded considerably. I abandoned my primitive thee-ocking and started trying to yelp, cluck, kee-kee, cutt and cackle. Never mind that many of my practice efforts fell flat; I had a sliver of knowledge, and I was trying to improve. And by that spring, I could yelp and cluck well enough to make a turkey gobble. I didn't have much of a clue about what to do after he gobbled, but I could at least prompt him to sound off.

At that point, I was probably still normal. I'd learned to turkey call at a level that would probably let me kill a hot bird now and then. Further, I didn't obsess about it, and when the season ended, the mouth calls went in the snuff box and were forgotten until the next season beckoned. I was content to be a turkey hunter of modest knowledge and even less skill, and although I'd rekindled some interest in calling, I wasn't keen on being a turkey caller.

Then it all went to hell. One of the editors of the turkey hunting magazine announced his retirement, and I was tabbed as the new guy in charge. Weeks later, I attended my first National Wild Turkey Federation convention and walked into an aural firestorm that set my imagination ablaze. I found out I was passable with a box call. I learned that my friction calling needed some work … OK, lots of work. I confirmed again that my mouth calling was laughable. And I realized I had no idea how to run a wingbone, trumpet yelper, tube call or scratch box.

Thus began the long, slow descent into madness. The next winter was spent yelping and cutting on an aluminum call I'd received at the show. Another callmaker had given me a scratch box, and I spent considerable time with that, too. Oh, and I had new mouth calls — so much for the worn-out diaphragms in the snuff box — to yelp on. By the time the next turkey season rolled around, I was a better caller. I wasn't good yet, but I was better. And I liked calling — a lot. In fact, I began to accumulate calls at a pretty good clip. Many were given to me by manufacturers so I could "test" them or use them in photos with dead turkeys. That vice was bad enough, but it led to an even more sinister temptation: custom calls. Collectively, these proved to be a cruel mistress, because as I acquired one or two, I wanted more. Each was unique, and every sound was slightly different. I was constantly looking for an edge, and acquiring several new calls every season seemed to provide one. During this time, I hunted quite a bit with some outstanding callers; guys with titles such as World champion or Grand Nationals champ on their resumes. These folks took calling to a level I'll never achieve but to which I still aspire. Every year, I'd listen to their chops and try to imitate them. And the next time we hunted, I'd hear their yelping again and realize I hadn't narrowed the gap that much. A little, perhaps, but not that much. These guys were artists, painting vast scenarios with sound. I was the kid with a putty knife.

Those great yelpers helped me along the way, of course. Sometimes, they'd listen to my calling and suggest ways to improve it. Other times, they'd just drop a hint or comment here and there. And now and then, they'd tell me to keep working on the subtle aspects of realistic calling. At some point, I realized everyone runs calls in somewhat different fashion — the way they grip a striker, hold a pot, stroke a box call or position a diaphragm call in their mouths. Fundamentals, however, don't waver. If you huff too much air across the reeds of a diaphragm, you just sound like a guy butchering a mouth call. When you press down too hard on that striker, you squeak the front end of your yelp and sound just like another hacker hammering on a friction call. Muscle memory from practice helps, but the lessons and adjustments are never-ending. If you're not getting better, you're getting worse.

And that is the mindset of calling insanity: constant devotion to the art and a never-ending quest to acquire better instruments. But when you realize and accept your own version of madness, does that mean you're actually sane, or does it indicate you're too far gone and cannot ease up on the throttle? Nowadays, 25-plus years into the insanity descent, cassette tapes and written product descriptions have been replaced by Facebook sound bytes, online audio/video of the past few Grand Nationals and Worlds contests and more YouTube expert calling instruction than you could watch in a day. A casual conversation with a better caller turns into a 45-minute question-and-answer session on the subtleties of the front end with a particular stretch of mouth call. And then, with that audio still fresh in mind, a week-long yelping practice routine ensues.

And then there are the calls themselves. Take the other day, for example. There I was, messing with friction calls and categorizing them as A-listers, which are models I'd happily run in public; B-listers, calls with which I'd hunt but would probably hesitate to use in a contest or seminar; and the rest, which, for whatever reason, never really struck a chord with me.

After an hour of sanding, conditioning, yelping and musing, I figured that I had more A-listers than I could probably use during a spring, even if I carried three each day. I certainly wasn't going to kill a turkey with each one — not unless I moved to New Zealand or somehow transcended to an almost unattainable level of skill and opportunity. Yeah, I'd killed turkeys with many of my favorites and had scored on multiple turkeys with my select inner circle of calls, but that just compounded the problem. If I had special favorites among my favorites, even some great calls would get left inside the wire most mornings.

It seemed kind of silly. I bought turkey calls because I'm obsessed with increasing the realism I impart in my calling. But I mostly bought them for their intended purpose: to call in turkeys. If I was full up with A-list calls, did it pay to get more? What about B-listers? When would they get a chance? Should I just ditch the C-listers? Sigh. I hadn't even reached into my stash of boxes, diaphragms, wingbones, tubes and other goodies. I worried I was a raving turkey calling loony and certified call hoarder.

I thought back to the brown snuff box of mouth calls and a crude box call I acquired about that time.

"You know, I'll bet I could take just those original calls and do fine this spring," I thought. After all, my old hunting buddy and three-time World champion caller Don Shipp usually only carried one or two calls afield, and turkeys everywhere tremble at his name.

Maybe that would work. OK, of course it would work. But why would I want to try such an experiment? Experience and conventional wisdom hold that gobblers often lock in on certain sounds or pitches, responding to those calls but nothing else. What if I lacked the yelper that could hit that magic note? What if I weren't adept enough at running a specific call? And what if I didn't have enough calls to sound like multiple hens or mimic a turkey fight? Sure, Shipp kills turkeys with one or two yelpers, but let's face it, he's Don Shipp, and I am not.

Then suddenly, my madness made sense. These were not just calls, and they didn't just produce turkey-like sounds. They were critical tools in the continuing quest for spring memories. Calling was not some secondary skill but the essence of the spring game — one of the very things that make us turkey hunters and not deer hunters just shooting something in the off-season. Too many calls? Too much yelping? An embarrassing obsession with the art and practice of turkey calling? Ha.

Yeah, I was normal years ago. But in retrospect, I'll happily remain in my new turkey calling version of normal.

* * *

4 CHASING BLUE SKY

The first gobbler I ever killed was a field turkey. Or at least he would have been had I let him walk any farther into the open. But I lucked into him as I sat along the edge of a corn field, and he died in the field, so he was a field turkey. And he also probably represented one of my career high points when dealing with field birds.

Any wild turkey is fickle and difficult to kill, but open-country birds represent another level of challenge and frustration. Or you might just say they're buggers.

Turkeys love fields, of course. After they're done with their roost trees for the night, they really don't need timber again until fly-up time. They can mill about a meadow, clearcut, pasture, prairie, hay field, stubble field or similar opening all day if they want. There's usually plenty of food in such spots, and birds can spot danger long before it reaches them. And hunters, I'm afraid, love fields, too. We know we have a good chance of encountering turkeys there. Moreover, we naturally like to see the game we pursue so we can watch its actions, determine its interest in approaching our setup and then get a clean, open shot. We do it with deer, ducks and countless other critters. To do so with turkeys seems intuitive. And maybe it is, except … the obvious dilemma with field turkeys is, well, they're out in a damn field. And unless the cover or terrain allows, you can't get close to them. Any ill-advised movement will immediately create another kind of field turkey — one that's moving swiftly elsewhere. If you can lure birds into timber or they feel like coming to a decoy, great. It happens. But it doesn't happen all the time, and field turkeys don't have to get within a country mile of your gun barrel. Worse, after they enter a field, they often don't want to leave.

Many smart alecks tell us the conventional wisdom for dealing with field turkeys is to leave the area and locate another turkey or find a good rest for a .223. The latter is no fun, and the former is easy to say but tough to do. After all, when you see a turkey in a field, you've already solved a large part of the hunting equation: locating a bird. And although there's undoubtedly a turkey somewhere that's easier to deal with, it's very difficult to strike out on blind faith in an attempt to locate that gobbler. There are no guarantees you'll find him. So we persist with open-ground birds. And if we fail, the field turkey provides an easy out. Hey, he was in a field. You did your best.

Technology has made things easier. Years ago, we didn't have pop-up blinds or ultra-realistic strutter decoys, both of which can be very effective for field gobblers. Many turkeys seem to pay little attention to camouflage blobs that appear overnight in open areas, and faux longbeards can often spark swift, violent reactions from toms hellbent on intimidating a rival. Still, neither method works all the time. So depending on the situation or your preferred style of hunting, you often end up back at square one — hunkered in cover, staring at a turkey in a field and trying to figure out how to reach him or lure him close enough for a shot.

Experience provides some potential solutions. Years ago, a turkey hunting legend led me through some lofty white oaks along the edge of a Kentucky hay field. The big timber hid our approach from a gobbler and his harem, and within minutes, we sat near an old logging road that provided a great ambush spot. To my astonishment, the hens led the longbeard along the field edge, and I shot him. Years later, I spied a lone Merriam's atop an open hill in South Dakota's Pine Ridge Sioux Reservation. Thick woods let me get within 120 yards of the bird, and then I slithered like a snake to where he'd been. I couldn't see the turkey, so I eased against a lonely cottonwood tree and yelped. The longbeard gobbled from 100 steps away and steadily walked to my call. My buddies, high atop a ridge a half-mile distant, watched the turkey topple over and then heard the shot echo across the prairie. It almost made me look competent.

There have been others, of course, but those stick out as benchmark field birds, and they represent a large part of my optimism with open-country gobblers. History repeats itself, after all, so I'm always trying to go Kentucky or South Dakota on any field gobbler I encounter.

Of course, not all experience is positive, and past hunts also plant doubts in your mind. I once dealt with two frustrating field gobblers for several consecutive days. One morning, I sat a buddy about 40 yards in front of me and then sat back to call. Astonishingly, the turkeys cut me off and raced to within 15 steps of my friend. I watched them strut back and forth, enjoying the view but wondering why he hadn't shot. Soon, the birds began to wander off. I yelped fruitlessly and whispered "shoot" as loud as I dared, but the hunt was finished. Later, my friend revealed he could have easily killed one gobbler but wanted the other, which had been obscured by brush, as he thought it had a longer beard. He hunts by himself now.

I continued to chase those birds for several days, often getting close but never close enough. One afternoon, I crawled along a small pine plantation, across a plowed field and through a thick fence line in pursuit of the rats. They just kept wandering along, and I ended up with aching muscles, an empty turkey tote and a neck full of ticks. Another day, I undertook a massive end-around and spied the birds loafing in a hay field with several hens. I resolved to be patient and let them make the first move, but I couldn't help myself. It's amazing how far turkeys can fly.

About a year later, I ran into another gobbler strutting for several hens at a nearby hay field. Timber provided a decent approach to within 100 steps of the birds, so I slithered to what I thought was a good calling setup and started yelping. The reaction was swift: The longbeard craned his neck at my yelping, slicked back his feathers, walked to the middle of the field and began feeding. Apparently, my seductive calling had made him hungry. All wasn't lost, however, as the birds were still out there. I observed them for a while as they fed north, away from me. But soon, some of the hens turned and started feeding toward the south. Their progress was slow but steady, and I figured I might get a shot at the gobbler if I could intercept their route to the woods. A long crawl/walk ensued, and I was soon propped against an oak, looking at the approaching turkeys. Again, I was met with a swift reaction. For no obvious reason, one of the hens stopped, looked to the west and then ran back to the middle of the field. The other birds followed. Coyote? Another hunter? Who knows? Whatever the reason, the turkeys were again several hundred yards away.

I considered leaving, but the birds seemed to settle down and resumed feeding in my direction. Uncomfortable and impatient, I watched as they picked and pecked to within 70 steps. It was going to happen. Then, inexplicably, the lead hen veered off to the west, over a little knoll that led to the woods. I wanted to move immediately but had to wait until the rest of the flock disappeared behind the terrain rise. When that finally occurred, I slipped out from my hide, snaked through the woods and peered up over a log ... just in time to see the gobbler and his hens drop down into a big ravine and out of my life.

My ultimate field folly probably occurred in Texas years ago. A buddy and I listened as 20-some Rios gobbled their wattles off on a ridge but then flew down the other way and headed toward a vast prairie to the south. We grabbed our gear and attempted to cut them off, but they had too much of a head start. Soon, we were glassing the open country, marveling at the multiple black specks 500 yards away. Having no better plan, we tried to use the grass for cover and slip closer to the turkeys, hoping some would filter back toward the timber that morning. To our credit, we never truly spooked any birds. However, it was obvious the turkeys knew we were there, and they always stayed several hundred yards in front of us, content to play cat and mouse all day, instinctively knowing they had the figurative high ground. Ultimately exhausted, we accepted our failure and retreated. Yeah, we should have left right after we saw the turkeys in that vast ocean of grass. But they were right there ... so close. And that was our downfall.

Too often, probably, we sit and watch turkeys do their thing in fields. We yelp. They gobble and strut. We crawl to the field edge and place a decoy in the open. They ignore it. We move. They move elsewhere. We wait. They stay. We plot. They foil. It's maddening yet wonderful; a grand gobbler tantalizingly close yet just out of reach, our minds churning to find a strategy to solve the puzzle. Often, we're stuck looking at the carrot with no way to reach it. Like the man said, "The view from hell is blue sky ... so ominously blue."

I'll probably watch the view again this spring. You will, too. Appreciate it. Enjoy it. Do your best to solve the riddle. End the day knowing you played the game as well as possible. There could be worse things than chasing blue sky.

* * *

5 A FOOL'S FORTNIGHT

It's never wise to become obsessed with one turkey. In fact, it's downright counterproductive if you're a serious turkey hunter. Focusing solely on a troublesome gobbler can lead to heartache and tag soup at season's end. Further, it might rob you of great experiences and adventures elsewhere in pursuit of more reasonable birds.

But sometimes, that old white whale digs its teeth ... er, spurs, into your soul and won't let go. Then, you've no choice but to see things through to the end.

Day 1: It was black-dark, and I really wasn't sure where I was. A friend had encouraged me to hunt his father's small woodlot, and I'd eagerly accepted. Trouble was, I'd only walked the spot once before, and that had been at midday. A fly-down hunt the next morning seemed ill-advised, but that's what I was attempting. If nothing else, I figured, I could hang back a bit and make it sort of a hunting/scouting mission.

Those thoughts vanished when the first gobble ripped through the cool morning air. My chin shot up from my chest as I tried to fine tune the bird's location. Another gobble followed, and I realized the turkey was about 100 yards in front of me but higher up on the ridge to the west. I wasn't in great calling position, but I was sure in the game.

After 30-some roost gobbles, the gobbler and several hens pitched down to the west, away from me, and seemed to mill about the ridge top. I called aggressively at first, but the gobbler only answered every third or fourth call. He was henned up, of course, so that wasn't a surprise. I tried getting a response from the hens for a bit, but that went nowhere, so I toned down my yelping and plotted a move.

"The ridge is wide open, but I might be able to slip around to the south and get on the other side of him," I thought.

It might have worked, too, had I attempted it immediately after flydown. That morning, however, the birds had too much of a head start, and they drifted westward before I gained any ground. My last yelps elicited a response from 300-some yards away, far off the property.

No matter. I'd located a bird. If he roosted in the same place the next day, I had a good chance of killing him.

Day 2: I got an earlier start and slipped quietly up the ridge, finding a tree that would probably put me within 60 yards of where the bird had been the previous morning. The turkey gobbled seconds after the first cardinal had sung, and I felt good about my chances. He was a little farther north but still fairly close. And if he flew down to the high ridge, he'd almost be in range.

No dice. The bird gobbled about half as much as he had the day before and then pitched almost straight down into an open bowl. One gobble on the ground brought a bevy of hens out of the surrounding trees, and the gobbler was soon surrounded by escorts. My calling netted almost nothing that day, and I really don't know where he ended up. However, I figured I needed to be farther up the ridge the next morning — almost under his tree, if possible.

Day 3: Another day brought another ridiculously early morning and tip-toe hike up the ridge. I'd arrived 15 minutes earlier than the previous day, hoping to get right under the rat and shoot him the second his scaly toes hit the dirt. As I settled my back against a tree, subtle drumming told me I was in his wheelhouse.

The first gobble was so close I almost jumped. The bird was probably almost in range, back where he'd been the first morning. There would be no calling until he hit the ground — just a gunshot. I sat and listened to the serenade for a half-hour or longer and was only moderately disappointed when I heard the harem of hens pipe up before flydown.

Without warning, a turkey fluttered down from an oak and sailed into the flat of woods to the south. Was that him? I waited. Two more turkeys flew down in that direction, and a gobble 100-plus yards away gave him away.

"Dang it," I thought. "Now he's going that way?"

I called quite a bit to the longbeard that morning, and he answered frequently. But he also made a big circle southwest and then northwest with his hens, moving almost out of hearing range. Then, as expected, he shut up and gobbled no more.

The bird had whipped me three consecutive mornings, and although the hunts had been action-packed, I was getting a little self-conscious about it. A turkey that roosts in the same spot day after day is telling you how — no, begging you — to kill it, yet I hadn't even come close. I vowed to change things up and do better the next day.

Day 4: Never had a chance. I slipped up the ridge like a coyote that morning and looked west toward what I figured was the roost tree. No one had informed the gobbler, however, and he was roosted 100 yards behind me at the base of the ridge. I'd walked directly underneath him in the dark. A brief battle ensued at flydown, but the gobbler and his hens walked off to the east that morning — across a brushy creek, mind you — and shut up early. This was getting embarrassing.

Days 5 and 6: Different days, same whippings. One morning, he was roosted over the open bowl. The next, he was back where he'd started. Both mornings, he gobbled his wattles off on the limb, pitched down with hens and left the area.

It was late in the season, and I really needed to pursue some other turkeys. I vowed to leave the bird alone for a day or two and see what I could do elsewhere. But I'd been so close so many times that it was tough to make myself do that. Surely I could kill a turkey that roosted in the same general area day after day.

By now, you've probably seen the obvious solution to my dilemma: If the gobbler returned to the woodlot every night to roost, he'd be relatively easy to ambush and kill during the evening. Trust me, I thought about it. Ultimately, however, I didn't want to end things that way. It would have been legal and mostly ethical, but I never tried it. Nope, I was in too deep, and I vowed to play the game by the rules we'd set.

Day 7: There's no debate: I should have killed him this day. Again, I unknowingly walked under him in the dark, as he'd roosted near the base of the ridge. But for once, his hens were roosted on the ridge, and he was alone. I realized that early and spun around the tree to face him. At flydown, he stopped by the base of the ridge, just 100 yards away but down a steep slope. I called now and then, and he answered almost every time. There was no need to overdo it, as his girlfriends were behind me. He would come up that ridge.

But after almost an hour, he hadn't. In fact, he stood almost in place, drumming and gobbling, waiting for hens to come to him. And my impatient nature got the best of me. "He's only 100 steps away," I thought. "If I can slip 50 yards down the back side of the ridge, he'll be in range."

So I stopped calling, placed my calls on the ground, wiggled out of my vest and started to creep down the ridge. The pace was agonizingly slow, as I dared not make any noise in the crunchy duff. I'd made it about 15 yards when I realized the turkey had stopped gobbling. I feared immediately I had spooked it, so I stopped and tried to assess the situation.

Seconds later, the gobbler's glowing white head popped into view as he ascended the ridge. In slow motion, I tried to swing and mount my gun toward him, but it was no good. He'd seen me instantly, and instead of reversing course, continued up and over the rise, taking flight when he reached the other side.

I'd had him. And I'd blown it. I'll spare you most of the details of **Day 8**, which was the final day of that turkey season. The bird was still in the woodlot, and he gobbled at me a bit. But he'd roosted off to the north and walked away to the west, leaving me more confused than ever about how to kill him. I left early that day and tried to find another turkey, but my tag remained unfilled. The woodlot turkey had kicked my butt all the way into the off-season.

Day 9, the next spring: It had been a great season, mostly thanks to good fortune and partly because I'd avoided the woodlot demon. But when my buddy told me the turkey — or at least one that behaved the same way — had returned to the ridge, I couldn't resist. I would atone for my shame the previous year.

Just not that day. As daylight finally began to break, I saw turkey forms in trees around me. Soon, the gobbler sounded off about 75 steps away. Another joined him from behind me. That was good news, as a subordinate turkey might make for a successful hunt.

All the turkeys flew down on the ridge and seemed to mill about for a while. The gobbler responded to a few of my calls but eventually drifted off, presumably with hens, to the north. The bird behind me never gobbled, but his drumming revealed that he remained fairly close to me for an hour. Eventually, I saw him slipping northwest, out of range and off the property. Another failure had come and gone.

Day 10: I decided to switch things up and approach the turkeys from the west instead of the east. What could it hurt? The walk up the ridge was easier, but it was also wide open, so I had to arrive ridiculously early, and I got turned around. At gobbling time, I realized I'd strayed far to the north, almost off the property. One bird gobbled from the ridge, but he never responded to my yelping and was too far to see.

So I sat dejected, thinking about other turkeys I should chase and wondering when I'd catch up on sleep. Then I heard a yelp. Peering through the woods, I saw a hen about 80 steps away, walking swiftly up the ridge top to the north. Then she ducked under the fence and disappeared. Two more hens followed, and then the strutter appeared, hot on their tails. I watched as he walked off the property and made a beeline after them. Minutes later, he began gobbling regularly from some unseen open area, almost out of hearing range.

Hmm. The birds had gone north the previous day, too. That almost seemed like a pattern, which the gobbler never exhibited the year before, when he'd refused to do the same thing two consecutive days.

Later, I reviewed aerial photographs of the woodlot and noticed a green pasture to the north. That had to be where the birds had gone. And if they were going there every day, I could put myself in position to intercept them. That afternoon, I returned to the woodlot, counted my steps up the ridge and then counted 50 steps east to a tree that sat right atop the ridge's high spine. The birds had to be following that around to the north on their way to the field. I'd wait for them soon.

Day 11: My arrival time was laughably early. After counting 150 steps north and 50 steps east, and taking several branches in the eye, I sat by the tree and wondered why any rational human would be in the woods at 2:30 a.m. Yet there I was, wide awake.

When hints of light appeared in the east, the folly of my previous 10 visits was washed away. Dark forms hovered in the branches ahead of me, and a gobble broke the silence just 60 steps distant. The bird hammered for 15 minutes and then flew down early. Several hens pitched toward him. Soon, a hen appeared off my right shoulder about 15 steps away, walking along the ridge spine toward me. Then the huge white head and broad fan appeared 30 steps behind her, directly down my shotgun sights. Normally, I would have let him approach a bit longer and clucked sharply to punctuate the hunt. That day however, he hesitated briefly at 42 yards and raised his head slightly. The shot string was already on the way.

As expected, the woodlot demon was an older bird, sporting a gnarly beard and 1-3/8-inch hooks. Standing above his still form atop the ridge, I thought about our many battles and the journey we'd shared. I was proud and thankful yet humbled and a bit regretful. The 11-hunt, two-season campaign was finished, and I was sorry to see it end.

Yeah, I know 11 days stretched across two springs doesn't represent a true fortnight. Details. After pursuing that bird for so many ugly-early mornings, my mind was a bit hazy, so the title made sense. And honestly, I'd have hunted him for 11 more days if given the chance.

* * *

6 GREASING THE HAND OF FATE

After a few seasons on your buttpad, you narrow down turkey hunting's necessities and begin to leave superfluous stuff at home.

Good camo and comfortable boots are musts. Calls, of course — enough to sound like multiple turkeys but not so many they become a burden. Weapon? Check. Decoys and blind? If you prefer. Snacks, water, binoculars, ratchet clippers and a good knife? Yep.

On the mental side, experience and patience are required. So is the knowledge that turkeys are capricious, unpredictable animals that might not cooperate despite expert efforts to do everything correctly.

For most folks, those items and that knowledge are enough, and anything more is excess baggage. Sure, you'll tote a few more tidbits along some days, but generally, basic gear and hard-earned wisdom rule the day.

Except, of course, when you consider chance.

Let me back up. I don't believe in fate or luck. I guess every one of us has a destiny, but we are firmly in charge of that path. Coincidence, irony and fortune often intervene, but we remain the lords of our fate until we die. So I guess it's especially funny that so many turkey hunters, including me, remain so tied to superstition.

There's the usual stuff, of course. If a black cat crosses the road in front of your vehicle, you'll probably suffer an unsuccessful day. Two birds sitting on a wire near your hunting spot? That's usually bad news, too. But my turkey hunting superstitions go a bit deeper and, possibly, run a bit more toward the absurd.

For example, when I hunt, the left boot goes on first and is taken off first. I'm not sure how I started this ridiculous ritual, but at some point, I noticed I seemed to kill more turkeys on days when I started with the left boot. It's not that I didn't score if I started with the right boot. I just wasn't quite as successful.

I'm kind of weird about shells, too. I carry as many shells as I want, provided the number is seven or four, with the former being preferable to the latter. Carrying six is still OK but not ideal. Having five is outright bad luck, and three or fewer is tempting the wrath of the gods. I probably started the seven-shell superstition because seven is typically considered a lucky number. Plus, it seemed practical: Three shells went in the gun, and four in the pocket gave me enough to fall back on if I shot poorly but not so many that they rattled around incessantly or became cumbersome. The four-shell superstition started on rainy days. I needed enough for the gun and at least one spare, but I didn't want to get any more ammo wet. The bad-weather component of that superstition is the sole reason seven-shell days are better than four-shell outings. Six is the iffy number. If I'm carrying a half-dozen shells, it usually means I've missed a turkey or killed a bird yet continued hunting. I've experienced some hallelujah days when I shot a gobbler early and went on to take another longbeard later. In such cases, six shells worked just fine. I've shot three birds in a day, too, but during those hunts, I usually restocked my shell supply at lunch and then carried seven into the woods for the afternoon adventure. Five shells? Bad news. That usually means I've missed twice or needed more than one shot to kill a bird. Or, perhaps I missed early but redeemed myself later. Either way, it's time to regroup. And carrying three or fewer shells doesn't make any sense, as you have no backups. That's just common sense (refer to the aforementioned misses).

The astute among you might wonder whether my good luck would remain if I carried seven shells into the woods but missed a gobbler three times, leaving me with four shells. Nope. Doesn't work that way. The only way that could pan out is if I left the woods and it started to rain, leaving me no choice but to go with the four-shell option the rest of the day. Make sense? Glad I could clear that up.

I'm also big on lucky tokens or objects, but that's tricky ground. You can't just grab a favorite wingbone, deem it lucky and then expect fortune to smile upon you. Instead, you must come upon these talismans innocently. Finding a turtle shell in the woods is a perfect example. That is fantastically lucky, and if you carry the shell in your vest, you're sure to score that day. The same goes for an American Indian artifact, especially a complete arrowhead. I've also been given several lucky items by friends and relatives. Again, you can't just wish that these tokens will bode good fortune; you must stumble upon it. During a particularly tough stretch a few years ago, my young nephew gave me a small plastic ninja toy to carry in my pocket, saying it would make me like a shadow warrior in the woods. I killed a gobbler the next morning. Nowadays, I am rarely without it.

Hats probably represent my greatest area of superstition. I never considered this until about 17 years ago, when legendary Alabama turkey hunter Bob Dixon guided me to a hard-gobbling longbeard in a deep swamp. As we shook hands, Dixon removed his camo cap and proclaimed it was his lucky hat for that season. The lid you wear when you kill the year's first turkey is your lucky hat, he explained. No exceptions. I quickly realized the cap I wore that day was my lucky hat for the year, and I donned it during every hunt that spring. Had my best year to date, too.

But here's the catch: When that season ends, the luck in your hat expires. You must find a new lucky hat the next spring, which can be tricky. You might start with an especially sporty cap or one that's very comfortable, but what if you strike out during your first trips to the woods? Sometimes, it's best to switch to another cap. Other years, the good fortune in the original cap might just be waiting to manifest itself. You have to proceed with caution in such matters. One rule remains, though: When you kill the first bird and reveal your lucky hat, do not deviate from it. Wear it no matter what. To do otherwise would sink your spring. A few years ago in Iowa, I struck a lonely afternoon gobbler and yelped him to the gun during a thrilling hunt. The return trip to the truck was long and hot, and when I ducked under the cattle gate by my vehicle, I accidentally left my hat atop a fence post. Then I drove 30 miles back to camp. An hour later, after cleaning the bird and changing clothes, I realized my mistake. I immediately drove back to the hunting area and breathed a huge sigh of relief when I saw the sweat-drenched cap on the post. I was late for supper that night, and a friend just smiled and shook his head at me when I walked through the door. I was unfazed. There was no way I was leaving my lucky hat in southern Iowa. Shoot, I might as well have taken a black cat with me the rest of the season and put my right boot on first. And carried two shells.

After reading this, you've likely concluded that I'm daft ... if not outright mentally ill. Luck does not exist — not in Vegas or in the turkey woods. If everything else is equal, fortune is swayed only by chance and coincidence. To think differently is foolish. I would be just as successful or unsuccessful if I wore a different hat each day and paid no attention to my boots, shells or plastic ninja. But turkey hunting can be rough on the mind and heart, I guess, and sometimes, a little encouragement or perceived advantage — no matter how stupid — can keep you optimistic. Really, there's no harm in that.

So I'll continue my childish rituals and carry my silly tokens into the woods, and I'll keep hunting hard, knowing that I've done everything possible to sway fate in my favor. Oh, there's one other thing I'll always carry, too: toilet paper. That's not superstitious. It's just common sense. Man, doing otherwise would truly invite misfortune.

* * *

7 MOONLIGHT MILE

If you hunt turkeys long enough, there will come a time when the birds on your home ground aren't quite enough. It's not that they're not exciting or challenging. You just ... well, you just want a little more. Different country. Varying hues or colors. New cultural experiences.

So starts the wanderlust.

It's not the fault of the turkeys, of course. I blame other factors. Maybe it's the well-traveled gent at an NWTF banquet who fills your head with tales of the Texas Hill Country or the Black Hills of South Dakota. It might be the magazine that arrives during bleakest, darkest winter, filled with gorgeous sunset photos and stories of far-flung pursuits seeking gobblers with strange-colored covert feathers. Or perhaps it's one of the legion of outdoor TV shows, many of which show gleeful, high-fiving hunters knee-deep in turkey feathers at some exotic locale.

But no matter how it happens, it will happen. At some point, you will decide you must travel to hunt turkeys. And then, friend, you've gone through the looking glass.

Oh, it will be innocent enough to start. After all, what's the harm in going south in early spring for a few days before the season opens in your home state? And what would be wrong with heading west one May after hunting has pretty much wrapped up in your neck of the woods? Shoot, if you live close enough to another turkey-rich state, you can border hop a few days here and there, too. A grand slam? Why not? Every turkey hunter needs one. And if you're going that route, why not a royal slam and world slam? Seems innocent enough.

Sooner or later, however, you'll hit the tipping point. It's much like the razor-thin line between a guy who enjoys a few beers on the weekend and an alcoholic who cannot function without getting his bag on. Yes, at some point, you'll realize that being a full-fledged turkey road bum lets you indulge your obsession to the utmost. Instead of a three- to six-week season, you're wide open for two to three months. And rather than being confined to familiar hills and hollows, you can yelp up birds in cypress swamps, rugged river breaks, sun-baked senderos or snow-topped Western mountains. Oh, and let's admit the obvious appeal: Traveling across the country can let you kill a hell of a lot of turkeys.

I've been there. I've been the high-functioning alcoholic — er, turkey travel-holic (though the terms are not mutually exclusive). My season has started in early March at some remote southern Florida swamp and ended 12 weeks later in the North Woods or the Great Plains. I returned home just long enough to throw turkey meat in the freezer, put Borax on beards and spurs, and throw piles of filthy laundry in the wash. Then it was off to the next adventure destination.

Along the way, life changes and priorities shift. At first, the chaotic airport lobbies and hasty rides to remote camps can be unnerving. The first trip of the season always put me out of my comfort zone, even if I was among friends or longtime acquaintances. I didn't sleep all that well. I just felt a bit off. But then, the first morning of hunting would arrive, and I'd suddenly remember why I was there. I felt like a turkey hunter again, even if I was at an area I'd never seen before with folks I'd just met.

And then, after a trip or two, the turkey travel addiction hit full throttle, and frenetic, running-ragged road life became the norm. After being home for a day or two, I was ready for another early-morning flight or marathon cross-country drive. My body became more or less accustomed to airport chow and fast food, and I felt at ease sleeping, for a few hours at least, in pretty crummy motels, trailers or campsites. (Of course, conversely, I was also treated to some swanky high-end places, too.)

At the end of the season, my yard resembling a hay field and my wife viewing me much like a slug that's eating her hostas, I'd figuratively collapse and breathe a sigh of relief. I was off the road and glad to be home ... yet the lure of the turkey trail still called. It was always there, from June through February.

The turkeys themselves beckoned me, of course, but it was more than that — new landscapes, different settings, excitement about the unknown, and an ever-shifting array of wild characters and big personalities throughout. And the tales — well, the wanderlust provided plenty.

There was that long-ago morning in the company of legendary hunters, listening to an Alabama bird gobble his wattles off while I tried to remain composed for my first-ever filmed hunt. I'd forgotten to load my gun right away, and then had to squeak a shell into the chamber while several gobblers tore it up nearby. After flydown, everything worked perfectly, with the three gobbling turkeys running to within feet of my gun barrel. The video man gave me the signal to finish the deal ... and then I shot the wrong bird.

Some years later, I stood atop a high Sierra Madre Occidental peak in Sonora, Mexico, on my way to my first and only Gould's hunt. Some friends and I had been delayed in Arizona and then missed our connecting flight from Hermosillo to Obregon. With no other option, we'd hired a cab to drive us to the tiny burg of Jecora. But after turning a corner somewhere near the middle of nowhere, flares popped up, and a dozen armed men surrounded the van. It was the middle of the night, and my friends and I were surrounded by Federales armed with machine guns. They spoke no English, we spoke no Spanish, and our cabbie seemed to sidle up to their leader and give him the down-low on the suspicious gringos. After an hour of searching our gear, they let us go. Or perhaps someone in our group figured out who to bribe. It didn't matter, as we weren't going to a Mexican jail. We reached the lodge safely, albeit at 4 a.m., ate some tortillas and then went hunting. Days later, we chartered a small plane for our return trip instead of driving through those damn mountains again.

Through my travels, I've somehow learned the location of the best upscale sushi bar in Birmingham, Ala. I've also found out that Transportation Security Administration agents will likely flag your carry-on bag if it contains a two-sided long box. (Junior agent: "What's this?" Me: "It's a turkey call." Senior agent to junior agent: "It's a turkey call ... you turkey."

And then there was the case of the flatulent guide. We'll call him Rick, because that was his name. He was a great guide; a real throwback cowboy who for years had delivered deer, elk, bears, pronghorns, turkeys and many other critters to satisfied clients in the Southwest. I met him while staying at a spike camp in a valley surrounded by majestic Sangre de Cristo Mountain peaks in northern New Mexico. I'd filled both of my tags the previous afternoon across the road from our camp, but I was itching to see some mountain turkeys, so I accompanied another hunter and Rick into the high country the next two days.

The first day found us in pursuit of a hot-gobbling Merriam's roosted in a distant ponderosa pine. We followed a two-track as far as possible and then side-stepped along a rocky incline toward the bird. The rocks didn't provide stable footing, of course, so we slipped and slid quite a bit along the way, and that must have "shaken something loose."

When Rick made his first strange sound, no one reacted. Hey, we were hunting and occupied with other concerns. When the second odd noise came forth, the other hunter and I glanced at each other but quickly returned to turkey mode. By the morning's end, however, the strange sounds had become common, and the other hunter and I could not meet eyes without giggling uncontrollably. I'm not sure if Rick knew or even cared. He was out to get the hunter a turkey, and any emissions along the way were just collateral damage.

Rick asked if we'd like to hunt with him the next day, and we gladly obliged. He was, as mentioned, a very nice guy and a talented guide. Still, when supper was served that night, the other hunter and I locked eyes and immediately smiled. We dined on a casserole featuring elk, onions and plenty of beans. The next morning brought another *Blazing Saddles* repeat and more muffled laughter. But that afternoon, the other hunter shot a gorgeous Merriam's strutter, and all flatulence was forgotten.

The incident provided a hilarious sidebar to the trip and my turkey hunting career. There are dozens more, of course, and only on the traveling turkey trail do you experience such tidbits. Sleepless nights, borrowed guns, hastily drawn maps, midnight trips to Wal-Mart to buy tags, encounters with unfamiliar flora and fauna, and even perhaps gassy guides in the Southwest — they're all part of the vagabond turkey hunter's world. Like I said, when you taste the first sweet drops of this travel intoxicant, you're hooked. Then you, as I did, must take it to the fullest, traversing the country for more gobbling fixes. Each trip only fuels the desire for yet another.

Eventually, you'll probably reach a point where you back off a bit and only venture on select journeys. And like me, you'll probably spend more time at home, realizing that familiar ground, old friends and family members are also among the greatest joys of turkey hunting.

Still, it might not take too much of a nudge to send you down the highway or toward a busy airport. Hey, you might be missing something out there, and there's only one way to find out what that is.

But if you're headed to the remote mountains of the Southwest, I might recommend some Beano.

* * *

8 THIS SHABBY SWINDLER

He didn't see the booger, but he could smell it.

OK, yes, turkeys can't actually smell, but the gobbler sure sensed something was amiss. And in that moment, with him alert and turning to depart while I strained to find a clear shot, the game was up. A quick head-bob sent him back into the Missouri creek bottom, leaving me exhausted, exasperated and befuddled. I'd played 99 percent of the game correctly but was leaving that pretty timber with an empty turkey tote.

"What … what happened?" I thought, pulling down my facemask and squinting in the face of the midday sun.

I'd moved through the woods with relative stealth. My calling had been spot-on, or so I thought. My moves had been logical and precise. I'd taken the few clues the turkeys had given me that April morning, and I'd formed a plan and executed it. Even when the gobbler waltzed in silently, I'd been ready, my gun following his bobbing head between the brush and twisted roots in the bottom. But then he'd stopped behind a brush pile, his noggin barely visible. Seconds later, he was gone, vanishing like a wraith into the oak/hickory maze from which he came.

So it goes in the turkey woods. We plan, scheme, practice and execute our chops with as much precision as we can muster, and yet we're often found wanting — defeated repeatedly by a capricious bird with a brain the size of a grape. The irony is we knew that going in, of course, and have already decided to accept those odds. Like someone said, "If you're afraid of driving home without a turkey, don't step out of your front door in the morning."

But that inherent uncertainty never stops us from trying to erase or at least reduce the number of encounters when, despite our best efforts, turkeys win. Every season, we go afield with fresh enthusiasm and optimism, armed with better equipment, sharper of skill and experience, and ready to make full use of our greatest — perhaps only — advantage over turkeys: our brains. We are determined to avoid mistakes from hunts past, and we are better prepared than ever to anticipate and react to any curveballs turkeys hurl at us. We are confident and resolute. If a turkey makes a mistake, we'll kill him. Shoot, even if he doesn't make a mistake, we'll probably kill him. We're apex predators.

Trouble is, turkeys have been evading apex predators for millennia. And based on current population numbers, they're pretty doggone good at it. The only predator that came close to wiping them out was us (man), and that was during a period of vast habitat degradation and commercial overhunting. Even then, the bird survived in pockets, seemingly biding its biological time until conditions allowed it to flourish again. Nowadays, with the voluntary restrains and principles of fair chase we place on turkey hunting, the birds again have an advantage — and they display it time and again.

Consider this common scenario: You owl-hoot in the black pre-dawn, and a gobbler hammers in response. Deftly and silently, you slip to within 60 or 70 steps of his roost tree and set up. Your first tree yelps are met with a savage response, and as fly-down time approaches, you determine the bird is alone. With your gun ready for a shot the instant the gobbler's feet touch the ground, you revel in your good fortune and smile at your prowess. And then the bastard flies down the other way. The next time you hear him, he's 150 yards distant and leaving in a hurry. Soon, he's in a faraway field with a huge passel of hens, gobbling at every crane, crow and cow but not budging.

Or how about this one? You slip along a pretty ridge, yelping now and then, trying to strike a hot bird. At 10 a.m., a longbeard hammers in response from a nearby flat. You course the gobble immediately and determine to get close. Using the terrain and foliage, you cut the distance in half, find a great setup and yelp again. Bam! The turkey is 75 yards away and seemingly closing. Up comes the gun, and you strain to see that light-bulb head pop into view.

After a few seconds of silence, you cluck and purr softly, giving the old warrior just enough incentive to come all the way in. Nothing. A few minutes later, you yelp softly and finish with an inquisitive cluck, hoping the bird will again reveal his position. Nada. You tilt your head to and fro, trying to hear drumming. Zero.

But you know he didn't spook. He didn't go anywhere. He must still be right there, playing coy. You vow to wait and use silence to pique his curiosity. Finally, after 20 or so minutes, you realize (duh) that the gobbler isn't coming. In fact, you don't have a clue as to what happened. You cutt. No response. You yelp and cutt. Zip. Then, ultra-slowly, you rise from your tree and peer through the woods. The timber appears to be empty. After five steps toward your truck, you hear a noise and cut your eyes to the right, just in time to see a gobbler flush, pump his wings through the timber and then glide a mile to safety. You then vow to take up another hobby — something sensible, such as building model trains.

Here's another. After listening to a gobbler strut for hens one morning, you sneak into the area and find a small oak flat torn to pieces by scratching. The next day, you wait in ambush there, vowing to let the ladies drag that gobbler to his doom. About an hour after fly-down time, you hear soft yelping on the ridge leading to the flat. You respond with some light yelping and soft clucking and purring. Two hens respond, and within minutes, you're conversing with them as they approach. After one series of yelps, a gobble erupts near the hens, and you're certain the entire breeding party will soon be in your lap.

Moments later, the lead hen pops into view, purring, scratching and pecking for acorns on the flat. Soon, two more join it, and you're pinned down by six turkey eyes. Drumming wafts through the air, and your eyes dart left and right to find the strutter. He will no doubt follow right behind the hens, appearing 20 steps from your quaking gun barrel. The hens continue along the flat, finally dropping off the edge on their way to a shady timbered bottom. The gobbler, his drumming still audible, is still out of sight but cannot be far behind the girls. You wait, ready. Then you wait some more. Soon, you realize (duh again) that your waiting has not produced any results, so you yelp softly. The gobbler responds immediately ... 70 yards away, with the hens that had just been in your lap. You remember something about model trains.

I could continue this forever. Likewise, you've probably experienced dozens, if not hundreds, of examples of hunts when your best-laid plans were thwarted because turkeys are ... well, turkeys. Not only are they maddening, but they seem to have a sick sense of humor about it. And, to varying degrees, they are like this from New York to California, and from Ontario to the Everglades.

Don't get me wrong. As I said, this does not mean we should accept defeat easily and simply play a game of attrition. No way. If we truly enjoy turkey hunting, we'll strive every moment of every day to be smarter, stealthier, sneakier, more realistic in calling and more responsive to subtle clues. In short, we're on a never-ending journey to be better turkey hunters. It's a huge part of the fun in this game.

We can succeed to a great extent, too. By learning all we can about turkeys, calling, tactics and our weapons, we begin to approach that apex predator status. By not repeating a mistake from a previous season, you might score on a bird that would have otherwise whipped you. By achieving ultra-realistic calling skills, you might pick up a few more chances. By capitalizing on every opportunity possible, you boost your batting average. Before you know it, your skills have let you kill a few more turkeys this season than the last. Through time, those birds add up, and you will have achieved "sho-nuff killer" status.

Ah, but even then, you won't — you cannot — kill them all. It's simply impossible, even for the best of us. When you do everything right to the best of your ability and still come up empty, that's when you must shake your head, tip your hat to the turkey and acknowledge that you'll never have a spotless record in the woods.

Perhaps Mark Twain said it best in his piece "Hunting the Deceitful Turkey," when he imagines what a hen might say to her brood while eluding a hunter: "I shall be back as soon as I have beguiled this shabby swindler out of the country."

So it will always be. We head afield each day, every season, armed with great knowledge and appreciable skill. Yet at any time, we might be nothing more than shabby swindlers attempting to peddle our silly wares to disinterested observers or birds that avoid us through unforeseen circumstance.

That's our game. We cannot hate that part of it while loving its more appealing aspects.

Besides, getting whipped makes for some great stories. And it sure

beats building model trains.
* * *

9 DEAD LEAVES AND THE DIRTY GROUND

The long-abandoned railroad bed stretched through the dark timber until it disappeared into a haze of green, gray and dark shadow. A thick, cane-infested swamp lay to the right, with a slightly higher bottomland oak/hickory forest on the left. Somewhere in that deep woods, two Alabama turkeys were gobbling, and a friend and I scrambled along the high tracks, lifted up 20-some feet from the rich Black Belt topsoil, to find a suitable spot to sit and call.

Moments later, with our backs settled against stout oaks and yelpers humming, we watched the pair of strutters march down the side of the railway grade, dart through the swamp and pop into the open 18 steps away. The end was thrilling yet almost anticlimactic, with flailing wings slapping the wet leaves as we celebrated.

I'd wanted to hunt the spot because the landowner said no one else had been there that spring. Fresh ground, I figured, is always better. Turns out that area had some turkey hunting history, though. Almost a century earlier, my host later told me, a fairly well-known writer had hunted that property and taken a gobbler or two. He later published an account of his adventures in an early-1900s outdoors magazine. Later, in the 1960s and '70s, when America's turkey boom was only beginning to ignite, other high-profile figures — notably legendary turkey killers Ben Rodgers Lee and Ben Ezelle — practiced their art in those bottomland woods.

Fresh ground? Not even close. It had just been idle for a bit before I got there.

That hunt changed my perspective about my place in the long

story of turkey hunting. It occurred when I was old enough to have a bit of knowledge about how to kill a turkey, the history of the sport and the bird's recovery from near extinction. However, I was also sufficiently young and inexperienced to think I was just part of a generation of up-and-coming turkey nuts riding the wave of population irruptions and the activity's burgeoning popularity. I guess both were true. Or neither.

But that trip and others that followed got me thinking about everything that had come before my small role in turkey hunting's tale — and everything that would follow.

Don't think I'm going to get all weepy about turkey hunting's past and potential future. I can't control my place in time, and I had very little to do with America's wild turkey success story. Actually, I'm damn fortunate to have stumbled upon turkey hunting when I did, when many similarly inexperienced hunters had been smitten by the call of spring and bird numbers everywhere were increasing and expanding annually. I was lucky to have caught the rising tide at a critical moment and can now relish what I believe is turkey hunting's golden age.

Still, some days in the woods find me thinking about how I got here. Every turkey hunter can thank American Indians and European colonists for making the bird part of this country's fiber. But let's face it, turkey hunting was pretty easy back then in the sense that humans weren't encumbered by the concept of fair chase and didn't limit when, where or how they killed birds. They saw opportunity for food or profit, and they took it. Yes, white settlers overdid it big-time, almost wiping out the turkey, but that's another story.

The generations I really admire were those that walked afield in pursuit of turkeys when there were only sparse, isolated populations remaining, and also the many conservation-minded folks who stopped the turkey's decline and later saw to its recovery. Without the latter, the story ends. That's it. And without the former, our knowledge of the bird, its habits and the skills required to pursue it might have disappeared.

Such thoughts also get me thinking about the almost ancient yet relatively unsullied activity of hunting turkeys. The calls we run are based on old designs that haven't truly been improved in decades. Our camouflage is an extension of concealment methods practiced centuries ago by American Indian hunters. The blinds some of us use are only handier portable versions of the hides crafty hunters used a century or more ago. Modern decoys look almost exactly like live turkeys, yet are they more realistic than the cape and feathers of a dead bird stretched over a form? I'll concede that modern guns, shells, optics and electronic devices have improved our success rate, but even those technological advances haven't changed the skills and methods of turkey hunting. Before Europeans colonized North America, turkey hunters had to locate birds, devise ambush strategies, mimic the bird's calls, remain hidden without movement and then execute clean killing shots. That hasn't changed.

Those skills were no doubt learned through generations of trial and error, with the lessons passed on from father to son, mentor to neophyte, for untold years, and then refined, perfected and passed on again. That ancient skill set existed when I took my first step into the turkey's world, and it will remain when I leave it. Hopefully, I'll have learned and honed many of those skills by the time I've yelped my last note. If not, I'll at least have spent my turkey hunting days in pursuit of that goal.

I'll just assume that turkey hunting's basic skills won't change much in the future, but I fear the world around the sport will. We have more turkeys now — 7 million plus — than have ever existed. Turkey hunting's ranks have swelled to more than 3 million folks, and you can pursue gobblers in 49 states and many areas of Canada and Mexico. It has never been better. Yet every year, the amount of land available for hunting shrinks — not in rivers but in drops, yet each loss is significant. As hunters compete for space and, more important, quality hunting, many will become discouraged. Privileged hunters will use their wealth to secure quality ground while excluding other people. I cannot blame them. It's their right to do so, and if they wish to pay for better hunting, more power to them. Still, hunters who cannot afford such luxuries will be left behind, and many will give up the sport.

Likewise, as the amount of hunting land decreases, so does turkey habitat. Every parking lot or pine plantation monoculture destroys wild ground and harms turkeys. I know all about the many urban turkey populations across the country nowadays, and I guess that's OK. It's a testament to the adaptability of the bird. Still, those turkeys are more akin to nuisance park geese or shrub-chomping city whitetails than the pure, utterly wild turkey.

I don't know how the tale will play out. I'll be long gone. Certainly, humans will continue to multiply and consume every available resource, often at the expense of wildlife and the total acreage of huntable land. Turkey hunting won't end next year or even 20 years from now. It and other forms of hunting will probably shrivel slowly and be available only to the rich, in time resembling the European model of hunting rather than the American ideal of wildlife conservation. I hope the history, skills and spirit of turkey hunting persist in those who choose to pursue the birds. As you know, the rewards are more than worth the effort.

"Whose woods these are I think I know," poet Robert Frost wrote a century ago — perhaps only years before the outdoors writer mentioned earlier in this piece chronicled his Alabama turkey sojourn. The famous phrase crosses my mind frequently while I'm turkey hunting nowadays, not regarding the timber I'm hunting but rather my tiny role in turkey hunting's epic tale. Whose woods? Not mine. I'm only here for a brief moment — a guest of the great folks who came before and hopefully a forebear of the many who will carry on after I'm gone.

* * *

BRIAN LOVETT

10 THE GOBBLER

Daylight was still just a hint, betrayed only by a pale eastern glow under the black dome of night, yet the gobbler had started another day.

With his feet wrapped tightly around the limb of a mighty white pine, the bird drummed softly, driven by instinct, lust and perhaps the dim recollection of hens that had flown to roost nearby the previous evening. Now and then, the abrupt scraping of wing feathers against wood confirmed the presence of other turkeys. Another chapter in a timeless spring ritual was set to begin.

But the day promised something different. Another set of eyes scanned the dark treetops in the pre-dawn; eyes near the ground, unable to pierce the darkness or focus on anything other than shadowy forms. The eyes, of course, belonged to a hunter who had silently yet inadvertently shuffled underneath a hilltop hickory within spitting distance of the gobbler. Neither knew of the other's presence, but that discovery would come quickly.

Sunrise continued its steady progression, and the gobbler felt energy surge inside his body. He'd experienced it before, when he'd been a jake and, later, as a 2-year-old, and its power always took hold of him during spring. Now, as an older turkey, his response to that drive was tempered a bit — not by wisdom or any human-like qualities, but rather a natural interpretation of his surroundings and his status among the pecking order of his peers. Still, as the electric sensation pulsed through the turkey like current from a capacitor, he tucked his head back briefly, stretched his neck forward and brought forth his first gobble of the day. The sound echoed through the woods and into the deep creek bottom below, announcing another dawn in the woods.

Soon, soft tree-clucks and tree-yelps floated from the boughs of nearby trees, and the gobbler affirmed he was not alone. Another tom sounded off in the distance, bringing a swift, primordial answer from the gobbler. Within minutes, the woods were alive with sound, as turkeys announced their presence and prepared to sail to the ground.

The racket had set the hunter's mind into overdrive. He'd lucked into a great morning setup and was determined to make it work. As quietly as possible, he eased his body around the tree so he faced the gobbler, which remained hidden amongst the pine boughs. Then, without thinking, he uttered three soft yelps on his mouth call. The turkey double-gobbled in response, maybe just in reaction or perhaps prompted by the new hen in his area. Encouraged, the hunter ignored his better judgment and called again, and the turkey reciprocated, fanning the hunter's hopes. His hands tightened around the gun's stock and fore-end, and his eyes darted left and right, hoping to see the bird fly down.

But the gobbler had already determined the outcome of the encounter. True, he'd responded to the yelping he'd heard, but he could also see several ladies perched on nearby tree limbs. When the first hen rose from her crouch, stretched her wings and then floated silently to the ridge below, the gobbler didn't hesitate. He peered at the open forest floor, barely visible in the pale light, hopped from the limb and flapped his wings until he touched down near the hen. Soon, other turkeys joined them, and like that, flydown was complete.

The gobbler stood still for a moment, surveying the hens before him as they pecked and scratched at the duff. Soon, one hen began to amble eastward through the open woods, on her way to a long, flat point that always caught the first warm rays of morning sun. Another hen followed, yelping softly as she went. The longbeard exploded with pent-up lust, firing a gobble toward the hens, his breath billowing steam into the morning chill. The fact that they ignored him meant nothing, and he burst into strut, tilting his broad tail fan this way and that toward the closest girls. And as they drifted away one by one, he followed, determined not to lose the precious companionship. Weeks in the future, he wouldn't care a bit about the hens and their broods, preferring instead the company of other male turkeys and areas rich in food. But now, his being was consumed by the drive to breed, and he was a slave to the urge.

The hunter, of course, could only imagine the scenario unfolding just out of his sight. He'd seen the birds fly down and had jumped at the tom's firecracker gobble on the ground. Still, he had no way of knowing where the turkeys were or where they intended to travel. He yelped on his call, hoping to hear clues in response. Nothing. Did that mean he was being shunned, or was the gobbler perhaps walking in silently? With no way to know, he grabbed another call, squeaked out some soft clucking and purring and then followed it with light yelps. Again, nothing.

That was troublesome. Only a fool would move in such a situation, not knowing precisely where the sharp-eyed turkeys had gone. Yet if he tarried long, the birds might drift away quickly, effectively ending what had been a promising hunt. Almost desperately, he summoned air from his chest and huffed it across his mouth call, sending a long, loud string of lost-yelps into the timber.

The gobbler, now almost 100 yards from his roost tree, raised his head at the calling but then immediately returned to strutting, spitting and drumming. A hen also heard the yelps and answered with aggravated cutting. With that, the gobbler could take no more, bellowing out another thunderous response.

The hunter faced a decision. The turkeys were obviously drifting away, so he had to move, but the open woods and dead leaves covering the ground would make that difficult. One misstep would send the turkeys scurrying or flying for safety. Cursing his fortune but deciding to make a safe play, he crawled away from the tree, ducked below a steep ridge line and then plotted a course around the turkeys. He could go no farther than the open point to the east, so that's where he'd make his stand.

The gobbler wasn't on the point yet, but he would be soon. Several hens had hastened their pace toward the flat, eager to munch on leftover acorns and fresh green shoots that grew on the old logging landing. The longbeard seemed content to bring up the rear, keeping the hens in sight and within hearing distance, yet acting almost disinterested while strutting and drumming. Only when a hen slipped out of sight did he quicken his step.

Soon, he'd caught up to the ladies, which had spread out across the open point, seemingly oblivious to each other and busy with their breakfast. This was perfect for the gobbler, as he could now walk among the girls, strutting for one that might soon agree to his advances, his brilliant back and tail feathers shining in the morning sunlight. There was no reason to go elsewhere, no reason to shout. He'd stay on that point with the hens until they left, and then he'd follow. If one would squat and indicate her willingness to breed, he would be ready. None did, but that did not deter his singular focus on the possibility.

Then suddenly, the dynamic changed. A hen far to the gobbler's right shot her head up and stared intently at a large pile of logging slash. Then, she putted once or twice and started walking away nervously, unsure of what she'd seen but certain it was dangerous. Other hens raised their heads and looked at their spooked flockmate. They hadn't seen anything out of place, but they were instantly on alert and ready to bolt for safety.

Having experienced this many times before — almost daily, in fact — the gobbler immediately morphed into survival mode. The desire to breed was almost overwhelming sometimes, but the will to live trumped all else. He stared at the spooky hen but then glanced at the brush pile. And when a slight, shadowy motion flashed near the slash, he needed no prompting. With several loud, hollow putts, he slicked back his feathers, dropped his tail fan and nervously rubbernecked west, away from the perceived threat. The hens followed, some flying and others running, and in seconds, the turkeys had vacated the point and were hundreds of yards from the source of their distress.

The hunter rested his forehead on the ground and cussed aloud. What a fool he'd been. With all morning to hunt, he'd rushed his pursuit of the turkeys and talked himself into a clumsy ambush attempt. The gobbler had been at the edge of range, but several hens had stood between the two, and their quick detection of his presence had saved the longbeard's hide. Knowing the gobbler probably wouldn't utter a sound for a while, the hunter rose, brushed the dirt and leaves off his belly and walked dejectedly toward his truck. Maybe he'd try another area, or perhaps he'd just take a nap. Either way, he wanted no further part of the henned-up old turkey. And he didn't plan on telling his buddies about his gaffe, either.

Meanwhile, the gobbler had settled down and resumed his day.

True, the close call had dampened his breeding desire for a bit, but it wasn't the first time his focus had been interrupted by a hopeful killer. Whether it took the form of a canine, feline, raptor or upright creature, predation looked the same, and his response never wavered. Flee. Survive.

But like most turkeys — even those that had beaten the immense odds of reaching three years of age — he quickly forgot the scare and went about the business of being a turkey. Several hens had flown into a dark, moist creek bottom, so he slowly walked toward the stream, picking now and then at anything that caught his interest. He didn't eat much during spring but took nourishment here and there as he could, often in the afternoons, when hens seemed scarce. And he didn't mind grabbing a sweet white oak acorn or two as he ambled down the slope.

Minutes later, the gobbler stood on the sandy shoals of the creek, peering into the woods on the other side. A soft noise caught his attention, and he craned his neck to listen. The sound echoed through the bottom again; soft yelping, perhaps from one of "his" hens attempting to find her traveling companions. Again, the longbeard's blood boiled, and he dropped his neck, lifted his feathers and strutted for a second by the water. When yelping again emanated from the woods beyond, he slicked down, walked back and forth a bit and then pumped his wings furiously until he'd cleared the creek and was near the hen. Still unable to see her, the tom stared for a moment and then, almost against his will, gobbled sharply. Two hens responded, and after a few steps, he was again at their side, strutting, drumming and following them through the timber.

So passed the morning, as the hens bobbed and weaved along the bottom, pausing at times to scratch at leaves, pick grubs or acorns and then walk this way and that. The gobbler remained with them in silence, save his drumming, usually strutting but pecking now and then at a morsel more out of seeming indifference than hunger. At one point, perhaps two hours after he'd reunited with the hens, he heard a crow sound off from a distant ridge. Loud, ringing yelping followed, and he raised his head to look toward the source. The noise continued for a bit, and it held his attention. Yet with his hens so close, the sound ended up being nothing but a brief distraction, and when it ended, he forgot about it and resumed strutting.

As morning gave way to midday, the sun shone hot, even in the deep creek bottom. Leaves once wet with morning dew became dry and crunchy, and streamside grass began to wave in the growing southerly breeze. Perhaps the hens grew warm or had fed enough, because they began walking toward a dense, dark grove of pines toward the base of the high ridge. Shadows never left that spot, and it seemed natural to spend the warm afternoon there, sitting, loafing or milling about until the cooler air of evening again prompted the turkeys to feed. The gobbler was also warm, his black feathers heated by the sun, so he did not hesitate to follow the girls toward the evergreens. He stayed there with them for hours, though he didn't reckon that, having no real sense of time. Instead, he sensed only that he was cool, with hens and not in danger. Now and then, he'd squat near the hens and remain still for several minutes. Other times, he'd rise, scan his surroundings and walk a bit under the pines, though never straying from the ladies. Once, he heard distant turkey sounds from the high ridge, but he remained silent. As before, the sound ceased and was quickly dismissed.

Hours later, as the sun began its slow descent westward and the air cooled somewhat, the hens stirred and left the shady grove, dragging the gobbler in tow. They walked slowly but steadily toward the top of the ridge, where a wide meadow stretched from the woods to a gravel hilltop road. There were green shoots, dandelions and insects in the meadow, and the spot was only about 200 yards from a point of massive oaks where the birds often spent the night. If someone had drawn up a turkey hunting playbook, he might have said the little field represented the perfect spot for birds to feed before flying up.

The hens topped the ridge after about 10 minutes of steady travel and then stopped to survey the field. A swallow darted here or there, and a lone Eastern bluebird zipped back and forth to a hollow fence-line box, preparing a nest. Otherwise, the meadow appeared to be empty, so the hens walked into the open and began feeding. The gobbler followed, pecking at the ground some but also strutting now and then for the hens. Three times, vehicles sped by on the gravel road, kicking up clouds of dust but continuing on. Every time, the gobbler raised his head to watch but never retreated. Had the cars slowed or stopped, instinct would have driven him into the woods, but he remained in the open.

That's where the hunter saw him, of course. After being soundly thumped at two other areas that day, he'd driven back to the scene of his morning humiliation, haunted by the memory of the henned-up longbeard and his ill-fated bushwhack. He wouldn't have paid any attention to the meadow, as it was probably a quarter-mile from his early-morning setup, but it was difficult to ignore two feeding hens and a lightbulb-headed gobbler 80 steps off the road. His foot hit the brake the instant he saw the turkeys, but then common sense told him to keep going, as if he were just a commuter hurriedly driving toward some important destination. When his truck was out of sight, though, he quickly pulled to the side of the road, grabbed his vest and gun and slipped into the timber. He had no idea the tom in the field was the same bird that had thwarted him earlier that day, and he couldn't have known how the turkey had spent the intervening 12 hours — the creek bottom and the pine grove — since their encounter. But then again, he didn't care. He'd located a longbeard, and he meant to have his revenge.

    The turkeys were about 250 yards from his truck, so the hunter crept quietly through the woods for a bit and then grabbed his binoculars and tried to peer through the timber. Nothing. He crept another 75 yards until he was within 60 steps of the field edge. Daring to go no farther, he looked through binoculars but didn't see anything. Hmm. Evening was nearing, so the hunter doubted the birds would retreat down the steep ridge. No, if anything, they'd probably fly up to some big trees along the slope and spend the night there. He was in good position but had to locate the turkeys, so he moistened up a mouth call, placed it on his tongue and lightly forced out five plain yelps. The gobbler, not 80 yards away but hidden by a subtle terrain wrinkle, heard the calling and immediately craned his neck. The hens acted disinterested and continued walking perpendicular to the hunter, toward a small copse of white oaks where they'd roost. The gobbler took a step to follow but stopped and looked again when he heard more yelping. This time, his pent-up energy could not be contained, and he responded with a thunderous gobble. When more yelping followed, he gobbled again.

    Optimism and desperation flowed through the hunter. He was close, but the time was short, and he wasn't going to wait on the old bird. With as much stealth as he could muster, he crawled through the open woods to the meadow's edge, using downed timber and thick understory vegetation as cover. When he was dangerously close to the field, his arms straining and sweat running into his eyes, he tried to calm his nerves and eked out three soft yelps. The gobbler erupted from 25 steps away, and suddenly, the hunter saw the grand turkey's white head, red neck and shining black body darting through the grass, looking to and fro but still following the two hens closely. No more calling. This was it. The hunter eased his gun to his shoulder, slipped off the safety and waited for the right moment. The gobbler caught the slight movement, took two steps and then held his head high to survey the situation, ready to flee.

Click.

The longbeard didn't need further proof of danger. At the sound, he bolted toward the timber and ducked inside cover. The hens were already there. The group continued along the slope of the ridge and finally stopped near some pines on a small finger ridge that jutted out from the main bluff. Then, as darkness consumed the timber, they flew up one by one, splintering branches and sending needles falling to the woods floor.

Furious at himself yet laughing, the hunter was already returning to his truck. He'd chased turkeys for years but had never forgotten to load his shotgun before. The gobbler had gotten under his skin twice that day, and haste and frustration had followed. Still, the hunter couldn't stop thinking about the thrilling encounters. He'd had the drop on the bird. He should have killed him but didn't. Tomorrow, he thought. The next morning, he'd walk in from the field and listen for the roosted turkey. Then he'd try anew to outsmart him.

Meanwhile, the gobbler sat in darkness on a large limb, watching, listening and oblivious to the hunter's plans. It was nothing new to have avoided another threat. Still, he would rest a bit before morning signaled a new episode, likely filled with more hens, other dangers and further reactions to the world around him. The gobbler had given the hunter a memorable encounter, but to the bird, it was just another day.

* * *

11 A FAR GREEN COUNTRY

Beyond sterile indoor scenes and dreary white or brown landscapes is a place you know well. It's a memory for much of the year, a hopeful destination through many long weeks and forever a calming retreat in your mind's eye. It's a vision splashed with color, but moreover, it's a canvas awash in sights, sounds, smells and a mindset. You've been there so many times you could find it in the dark (in fact, you have), and you will be there again soon enough, God willing.

Yet for now, you sit locked in the seemingly endless repetition of winter or summer, thinking back mostly about encounters past and gobblers battled, or dreaming ahead to fresh, verdant scenes and the promise of turkeys anew. The off-season is a tricky place to navigate, and you'll only steer straight through by keeping one eye on the past and another on the promise of spring eternal.

At first, it's not that difficult to step back from hunting and slip into down time. Turkey season, after all, drains you physically and mentally. (And by "season," I don't mean a few hunts here and there. I mean a full campaign that stretches from the first day you can get into the woods until the hour your last tag expires. You don't earn your official turkey bum card by hunting a few days and calling it good.) Long strings of ridiculously early mornings exact a heavy toll after several weeks. Burning climbs up high ridges, long walks through endless timber and marathon drives to new destinations further drain your batteries, and the emotional ups and downs from turkey hunting's inevitable peaks and valleys leave you spent. At season's end, beaten down yet immersed in the hunting lifestyle, you often reluctantly admit you're ready for the finish line. You have fresh memories and, hopefully, fresh turkey breast — enough of both to see you through for a while. And while you've indulged your annual obsession, life has continued around you, so you're probably behind at work and home, not to mention in a serious deficit when it comes to good will on both fronts. It's time, you figure, to find some closure with one season and start the journey to the next.

The first few days seem odd. Ideals you forsook weeks earlier — sleep, duty, fitness, sound nutrition, mental health — creep back into your existence. You clean your guns, repair and store gear, wash mud- and blood-stained camo and take a long look back at what worked and what didn't. You're happy and perhaps satisfied, yet you remain a ruthless self-critic, resolving to be better next season and perhaps taking a few steps toward that goal. Meanwhile, the campaign hasn't completely released you from its tendrils. You're obliged to report on your efforts, whether in person or electronically, and summarize your campaign to like-minded turkey folk. That might involve a bit of bragging or crying in your beer, but you at least need to tell your turkey brethren about your complete commitment to the cause and lifestyle. They, in turn, want to tell you, and unlike with shared tales in other hobbies or disciplines, you're both actually interested in hearing every account. You have other duties, too, including thanking landowners in person and with small tokens of your appreciation. It's only right to let them know what you experienced at their properties and reaffirm how much you appreciate and enjoy the privilege. There's an innocent ulterior motive, too, as the end of one season is really only the beginning of the next.

As the days pass, the next season doesn't enter your mind just yet. You slowly slip back into real life and enjoy it. Days and weeks flow by, and before long, you find yourself in full recovery from the season. Other events and pastimes fill your days, and you realize you're more than a turkey hunter. You're a husband, father, employee, boss, friend or teammate, and you happen to hunt turkeys.

Visions of the woods never completely leave your mind, of course. You might see a bachelor group of gobblers on your way to work or stop the truck for a family flock of hens and poults to cross the road. Maybe you run a call or two during a moment of down time or glance up at a beard display in your basement workshop while procrastinating about a project. But then life calls you back, you're reminded that the season is long finished and you're suddenly not solely a turkey hunter again. This cycle continues, seemingly endlessly at times.

But at some point, a long-dormant virus stirs, awakens and, as viruses do, begins to spread. Perhaps a chat with hunting buddies is the catalyst. Or maybe it's a few images in a hunting journal or even an outdoors television show. Whatever the impetus, the bug is back, and it grows hungry. The calls come out, and yelping again reverberates through the house. Maps or Google Earth images are strewn throughout the den, and a hunting journal sits atop the desk, opened to the account of a landmark day afield. Soon, magazines and catalogs arrive, and the Internet grows busy with a din of turkey chatter. You mark calling contests and other turkey-related gatherings on your calendar, and scour the freezer to make sure every scrap of the previous year's harvest has been put to use. Tags and permits begin to pile up, and the planning stage hits high gear. You contact friends, acquaintances, outfitters and other turkey folk, if nothing else just to chat about the upcoming hunt and build the buzz. It feeds the obsession but does not satisfy it.

Only one thing can do that. Your thoughts drift back to a familiar landscape — maybe a bit hazy since your absence but still vivid — that represents not only an actual place but an ideal or a composite of hopes; a goal that demands your attendance but much more. Soon, it begins to take shape anew in your daydreams. The weather is warm, but not too warm, with the sun heating the landscape just enough to dismiss the night's damp chill. The woods before you are a patchwork of brown and green, interspersed with dots of brilliant white or yellow. A chisel-plowed stubble field stretches off to your right, and an emerald pasture beckons to your left. The unmistakable smell of fresh-cut hay drifts by on a light breeze. The sky, once dark or steel-gray, shines blue from horizon to horizon, with only a light white cloud here or there to break it up. Your ears are filled with sounds, but it's not necessarily turkey talk. Returning songbirds tweet and chirp about, and a rooster pheasant might crow in the distance. Sandhill cranes and Canada geese pass overhead, calling loudly for reasons only they know. Somewhere, a tractor fires up, or a milk truck chugs away from the barnyard. A deer snorts at your clumsy intrusion, and squirrels skitter across the duff in search of mast. Your back is wedged firmly against a medium-sized black oak, your left leg bent upward and the familiar heft of gun and sling resting across your knee. A pot call sits on your lap, and your right hand dangles the striker while steadying the gun. You'll call soon, but not just yet. In a minute. It's important to get settled, of course, but taking in everything is paramount here.

That's your place. It exists in reality, and you'll get there soon during your renewed quest for spring. But it's every bit as real in your mind and heart as the vision or representation of all that is turkey hunting. You'll get there soon, too. At some point, dream and reality will meet once more, and you will truly be turkey hunting again. You might exhale a sigh and appreciate the annual cycle of life that day, or maybe you will just smile slightly underneath your facemask and thank God you made it there again. Whatever happens in terms of hunting — silence, exhilaration, disappointment, boredom or just a few hours outside — is immaterial. You will have returned to that green country and resumed your place as a turkey hunter.

Sometimes, the wait to get there is agonizingly long, and you wonder if you'll make it. But then you realize that little patch of real and figurative earth is always with you and has been since the first day you ran a yelper and lost part of your soul to a maddening black bird. And with that vision in your memory and future, a turkey hunter you will forever be.

* * *

ABOUT THE AUTHOR

Brian Lovett has been an outdoors writer and editor for 26 years. More important, he's hunted turkeys for 27 years, with the pursuit taking him to 20 states and Mexico. Along the way, he's recorded several grand slams and a royal slam, and has been whipped by more longbeards than he can remember. Lovett served two stints as the editor of *Turkey & Turkey Hunting* magazine, from August 1994 through January 2002 and again from November 2008 through the magazine's demise in March 2013. Between those runs, he was the editor of *Outdoor World* magazine and then *Gun List/Gun Digest the Magazine*, while remaining a contributing editor to T&TH. He's also written or compiled four other turkey hunting books: *The Turkey Hunters*, 2003; *The 2005 Turkey Hunters' Almanac*, 2005; *Hunting Pressured Turkeys*, 2007; and *Hunting Tough Turkeys*, 2010. Currently, he serves as field editor for the "On the Hunt" section of the National Wild Turkey Federation's *Turkey Country* magazine. He lives in Oshkosh, Wis., with his wife, Jennifer, and their dogs, Birdie and Buster.

Made in the USA
Columbia, SC
09 July 2021